Poetry My Love

Complete Poems from Soliloquies & To Poetry with Love

Gloria Edokpa

BOOK 1

Soliloquies: A Poet's Odes On Love, Life and God

By

Gloria Edokpa

MYSTERY

Everything is not as it appears

Nothing is as it is

Neither is anything as it should be

What is it that you seek?

What is it that you have chosen by your will?

That which you seek comes from the desires of your heart

& it is that which will rule you

That which you choose willingly

Comes from knowledge or ignorance of your 'All'

& it is that which will consume you

to save or to brake you

Do not attempt to make sense of my words

Else your blindness should consume you

Instead let my words consume you

& give you sight, you never imagined possible

Love is Life

Love is Life & life is love

My love is you & your life is me

Together we will bear sons of light

Children who's light will never fade

Sons & daughters who will never know death

for in us the curse will be lifted

what curse? i hear you say!

The curse of separation

The curse of blindness

The curse of wandering anti-clockwise

The curse of our fathers & they that were blind

For the curse isn't truly a curse but a clue

A clue to a blessing long foretold but forgotten

It is the clue to a land of great wealth

a land of great wealth long forgotten

What is this clue? i hear you say!

"That which you desire to rule will rule you

that which you serve will serve you

& give you a drink from it's fountain"

It is servitude that saves

it is the lust after kingship that destroys

Do not be troubled my love

The words that i speak to you carry life not death

Remember all is nothing & nothing is everything

left is right & right is left

nothing is all that it is

& everything is incomplete

This is a blessing my love

In love i 'Will' to serve you always

In love you 'Will' to serve me for always

In this love we have found life

This life we have found will reproduce itself

together we will rule in servitude to each other

together we are kings

together we will find beautiful treasures locked away

together we will watch our sons & daughters live forever

the key is love & trust

so if you love me

then trust even as i have loved & trusted you

My Love

If I told you the sun rises & sets in your eyes

Would you believe me?

If I told you the moon in all its grandeur couldn't compare to your beauty

Would you believe me?

If I told you I lived in you & through you

Would you understand?

If I told you I lived for your love

Would you understand?

If I told you I am you & you are me

Would you understand?

If I told you your eyes are mine & mine yours

That your lips are mine & mine yours

Would you concur?

If I told you that my heart is you as your heart is me

Would you love me then?

If I told you the moon & stars cry out for our love

Would you understand?

Watch the flowers my love

See them die in the winter

See them regenerate in spring

See them bloom in the summer

Watch their fall in the autumn

When we fight my love, it is winter

When I say 'I'm sorry' it is spring

When we make love it is summer

When we go to bed, it is autumn

& tomorrow my love, I know the winter will return

PS

I love you with all that I AM

Love's Salvation

In my day of trouble I called upon MY LOVER'S name

He heard, he came & rescued me

from the gloom that sort to obliterate me

Though everyone deserted me, he came for me

Though I was not worthy that he should come,

He came because he loved me

He came that I may know the true meaning of the word love

For though I have failed him on countless occasions

He sort to teach me that love is unconditional

It sees no fault

It sees no flaws

Remembers no wrongs

But most of all, stands faithful in the face of unfaithfulness

Now I know God is Love & Love is God

Undying, unending, flawless, pure, beautiful, peaceful, kind, gentle

If I could stay in love forever

Then it would be all good

Letter to My Lover

I wanted to send you a text but a text wouldn't hold all that i have to say

I wanted to call, but i fear that i might err by my words & end up sending you a smoked screen

I write because my heart is troubled

I write because my love for you gives me great unrest

I am divided in my thoughts

I am divided because even though i have given all of my heart to you

you have held back a bit of yourself & caused me to question your intentions

Time & time again i have held on to your words even though i see their emptiness

time & time again i have held on,

hoping & praying you will someday send me a word you intend to fulfill.

But i see now that day may come a little too late.

I think the circle of your empty promises has just about worn itself out!

You see my love, I know you better than you think i do..

Even better than you think you know your- self.

You laugh at my words now but look deep within yourself & you'll see that the words i speak are true

Maybe incomplete! but True!

pay close attention to my words else you get the wrong message

My words today are not to make you think less of yourself

or to create some false illusions that i am better than you or you better than i...

You think of yourself as smart, but this is not so

for smartness is not as it appears & foolishness is a mystery

I see through you my love & see that your ignorance is remarkable.

I see through you & i see how empty your brain has become

I see you & i see how you struggle to spell or stay focused long enough to shove a book down your empty brain

I see you & I see how you put up a shield

You wear a mask to cover your emptiness

Yet in your emptiness & Dullness i see beauty

I see how much of a child your emptiness makes you

i see how your weakness makes my love for you unconditional

No one can or will love you as i have

No one will come close to loving another as i have & do love you

My love for you is pure, flawless & unconditional

My life has become a sacrifice to you

But my love for you needs to grow,

it needs to breath,

it needs sunlight,

it needs an atmosphere good enough for survival

There's only so much blows my love for you can take before it becomes squashed

There's only so many cans of empty promises my love for you can drink

Before it starves & dies a gradual but painful death

My love for you starves for something that your foolishness cannot provide

So my love, if you will not save our love,

then i have no choice but to take my life from you

& retreat to the shadows

Watch me leave you today,

not because i have stopped loving you

but because i would rather you learnt the truth

the truth about the mystery of life on your own

lest my love for you dies

& there's nothing left between us

but emptiness

I leave you today not because i think less of you

or see myself in anyway better than you

I leave you today because i can see what you do not see

without you i'm nothing but a blind servant

However, even a blind servant has a wealth of hidden riches

-- Farewell my love --

Love's Enchantment

My Lord once said to me;

'how is it that you have enchanted my heart my beautiful one'

i answered & said;

'My Lord & my Love,

it is you who has enchanted my heart & everything that is me.

I am but a lowly poet & i know nothing of enchantment

I know nothing of mystery

& i know nothing of magic.

it is your love that fills my heart & makes me who i am

it is your love that inspires my pen & makes me write

it is my love for you that consumes me & makes me love even a stranger'

My Lord gazed at me & said;

'it is your love for love that enchants me my lover

it is your heart that puts a smile on my face

it is your labor for love that gives me rest

even so, it is in you i find a home'

when i heard these words that my master spake my eyes welled up with tears

my heart grew even more with love

so much so that i could feel it braking

then i said;

'my Lord, by my will i have chosen to love you for always & forever

even till eternity

in chains & in freedom will i love & serve you

in this world & in the next will i abide at your feet

upon your bosom have i found my rest

this love i have found is good

even so i will love everyone you give my way

i will show them how beautiful thou art'

Love's Lust

I once loved a man

but he wasn't mine to love

still, i loved him anyway

He's eyes were like a million rivers

& a million waterfalls coming together in one beautiful display of splendor.

& when he smiled,

his smile was the most beautiful sight i had ever seen

like an angel's paradise

only imagined in fairytales

his smile is the most beautiful sight you could ever imagine or see or dream

I loved this man

but he wasn't mine to love

so i could not speak of my love.

he called me his lover

& i called him my baby

if only i could,

i would suckle him at my bosom for all of eternity

but though i love him

he's not mine to love.

My love for him

is the sweetest taboo.

I would give a trillion treasures for the kisses of his lips

i would give a million rubies to feel his breath against my neck

Just to hear him say;

Mon Cherie Amour, i would give all of me

to feel his body against mine just for one more time

i would give anything.

my loins moan for him,

my body aches & moans for my lover

but the love i feel is cursed.

I loved a man, he was my lover, but he wasn't mine to love

so i let him go.

Mind

Man's mind is the greatest of all creation

It's likeness is that of a great King or a GOD

The unseen ruler of all

A king is not a king without his people

Neither is the mind anything without the body

A king is not a true king till he rules out of love & with wisdom

Likewise it is out of love & by wisdom that the mind rules

If the mind is the ruler

Surely the body is its people

With the mind men have moved mountains

With the mind men have taken many captive

With the mind men have led themselves down many dark roads

With the mind many have been dragged down the wrong path

But even with the mind, many have given love, life, hope & pain

If a king knows himself & feeds himself he will wax strong

if a king knows where life & treasures dwell

he will seek it out & conquer it for his people

If the mind cannot rule itself

just like a bad king it will seek to rule elsewhere

it will seek to rule others as a tyrant

it will aim at the thrown of other good minds to overthrow them

Yet even the mind is terribly cunning

capable of deceiving even its own self

if it does deceive itself

what else is there but to deceive another

A defective mind is one that is ignorant of itself

or has been deceived by another

it is infectious, wild & spreads like fire

Yet as the kingdom of a bad king does surely come to ruins

& his treasures fall into the hands of strangers

so too does all that belongs to the one with a defective mind

Chaos

Chaos is the mother of all

Indescribable, ineffable, incomprehensible Nameless, Unknown & unseen
Inconceivable, yet the conceiver of all that is

Without order, yet the mother of order

By her will she serves.

By her passion she rules.

Her will is love unconditional

Her passion is life

Her mind is her will

Her word is her passion

In her mind is love unconditional

In her word is life

Adam was a fruit of her love

When Adam erred, his err was by his will & in his passion

By his will he turned away from her word

In his passion he desired to rule her

Does a servant rule his master

by knowledge or by ignorance?

Adam failed to understand this mystery

It is the servant that is the ruler & the ruler the servant

Yet it is chaos that is both & all

She is fearful & dreadful

yet loving & sweet.

If Adam should look forwards or backwards,

she is there & everywhere

Both to serve or to rule

If she serves him, life will be in his bosom

If she rules him, like passion; she will consume him

Either way, Adam is helpless before her

Her will is to perfect him

If she consumes him out of his error

She will suck the life she gave him

& cause him to be reborn

Like the seeds of a ripened fruit

until he is perfected as she had originally conceived him

By your will,

you choose to love unconditionally

This is your servitude

By your passion,

the one you serve willingly will rule you

This is your desire to rule another

When love becomes your master

Chaos will find rest in you

She will find rest in you & serve you

She will birth order in you & cause you to become a great king

You will become the 'He that truly rules All'

A true King

A son of God

For a son's inheritance is his father's throne

& a servant seeks nothing of his master's

Mystery of Existence

A lie is not a lie

& truth is incomplete

A lie is an illusion

& truth is inconceivable

except it is revealed

A lie is conceived in the mind of its bearer

therefore has the potential to be revealed

I'm not right, neither are you wrong

We both see the picture from different angles

But with your view & mine

We can make the puzzle of life one big picture

A soft tongue turns away wrath

Like water on fire

But if fire meets fire who suffers

Is it you or i?

Perhaps both!

It is I that is your lover & savior

Likewise it is you that is mine

If I leave you to burn

Who shall save me

The servant is bound to his king

& the king to his servant

For both shall love & serve each other equally

Wisdom is incomplete without understanding

Understanding is fruitless without wisdom

Wisdom is knowledge

Knowledge of truth

Knowledge of the beginning

For it is only at the beginning that one can see the path of life clearly

Knowledge is life, love, God, health, science

Knowledge is the cosmos, plants, animals, me, you

Wisdom is knowledge of ALL

(the ALL of Existence)

How shall I know the All of Existence?

Given that I am not it but a part of it

Perhaps that's why I need you

Because together we are the All of Existence

If I loose even one of this little ones

Then my wisdom is incomplete & my understanding is weak

Wisdom & understanding in its fullness is like a beautiful mansion

The likes of which its beauty & splendor no eyes have seen

It is indestructible, perfect & without flaw

This mansion is immovable

How shall I see this great treasure again?

Perhaps you could help me

Together we can find this mysterious land

So hidden from our eyes

This land of our fathers long forgotten

In The Shadows

I looked back on history

and saw my brother's sins

I looked back on history

and saw my father's creations

I looked back on history

& stood transfixed

The sight I beheld altered my perception

The sight I beheld sort to recreate itself in me

since those before me are no more

I feel lost

Should I trust my father's creation as truth?

Should I hold fast to the unrevealed

& begin recreating life for those that I love

Have they that were before me loved me?

Or did they feel trapped in a loveless world?

Perhaps the creations of their hands were made out of ignorance

Surely if they loved me

I would behold that love even now

For love never dies.

I even I, feel lost in a loveless aeon

I fear that it is not only I who sees & feels this truth

I fear that those before felt this very same way

And these fears of mine make life nothing more than an empty circle

Alas I see a shadow lurking behind this image of gloominess

What is this I see?

lurking in the shadows?

It is beauty that surpasses my comprehension

Oh why does my heart skip at the thought of such beauty?

If history tells me that the imaginations of mans heart

Have been nothing but continuously wicked

Then let it be today that this beauty will be the imaginations of my heart continuously

My heart dances at the thought of such beauty & such hope

Do not hide thyself in the shadows away from my eyes oh beautiful one

Why have you hidden yourself in the depths of my heart?

Is it so I may search for you in all the wrong places?

Show thyself oh beautiful one,

for my heart desires thy presence

Show me thyself

that I may know the hidden treasures of this land

Show me thyself

that you may reveal the mysteries of this strange land

Show me thyself

that I may know that which is hidden from my eyes

Show me thyself

that I may rule & be ruled in love

Existence

In the Beginning was Existence

Pure, flawless & endless.

Existence is existence

& there is no non-existence.

For it is only in forgetfulness of Existence can non-existence be born

Suddenly formlessness took form& man had created a whole new world of form

A new world were existence in man had a counterpart: -non-existence.

what was one became two

& non-existence wished to continue existing

so it reproduced itself

it continued to shroud man's mind

& keep him sinking deep in the sea of forgetfulness.

a world ruled by darkness

where man bowed before the works of his hands.

But the All knowing is loving & knows all,

He sent a light that burns brightly.

My message is not one of condemnation

but of Love so pure & flawless the heart cannot contain it all

my message is not of an End

but a beginning so bright, pure, beautiful & endless,

it brings nothing but endless tears of joy.

My message is of Existence

& there is No non-existence

All that is born from existence is Good

& all that is born from non-existence is the opposite

when the sons of existence awake from their slumber of forgetfulness

they will exist

but when non-existence awakes

it cannot exist for it is not.

so it fights to keep the sons of existence roaming in a world of forgetfulness

through deceit.

for it is only through the existence of the son of existence in a world of
forgetfulness that he can exist & reproduce itself through evil

Existence beheld itself & willed itself to be.

This is the beginning,

Existence itself contains all but none can contain it all.

When existence willed himself to be

Then the father was

Though he always was & is.

The father willed his love be shared abroad

So man was born with the father in him but unable to contain all of the father,

he was given clairvoyance as a consort but clairvoyance was cunning

Even though she showed him the road to becoming like the father

she made him conceive separation.

But Separation meant forgetfulness

Hence Non-Existence

This Generation

I see a woman

Full of life

Beautiful, strong and caring

She is fertile and bears much fruit

Her kids are so diverse

All different colors, shape & personality

Black, white, colored, round, fat, skinny, tall, short

Each one unique in their own way,

and for this & more she loves them to death

Yet each one without an understanding of her unwavering love for them all

Selfishly seek a greater share of her love and comfort

In greed one child is turned against another

Black against white,

fat against thin,

red against pink

With the foolish thought that one is better than the other

I see her collapse from the confusion and war amongst her beloved

Slowly, her beauty disappears

Slowly Her life is drained

And her young children are left with no one to protect them

She drops to the floor bleeding and begging for help

But amidst the noise, only a few hear her cry

Some hear and listen but do nothing

Some try to make a change and fight for her to the death

Some go totally deaf to her cries

Some hear and choose to ignore her

What they fail to realize is

She's the very life they live

If she dies, they all die

If she lives, she protects them like a lioness protecting her cubs

Where do you stand in a world where love, unity and peace
have become mythical words?

Where do you stand in a generation where selfishness has become the norm?

Where do you stand in a generation where true love has become a chimera?

Where do you stand in a generation where innocent children are left with no
homes, no mums or dads but a cruel society?

The choices we make carry a cost, a trade-off and a benefit

Weigh the options involved with every decision you make

Ignorance

If life is bliss & my desires are for good only

Then where has the corruption called 'evil' sprung from?

Is it I that has created this hideous creature?

Or is it they that were before me?

Does knowing its origin really matter?

Or does it matter that my desires are for what is good & goodness only?

Can I have knowledge without ignorance?

Or shall I wait till the end when I will know all?

when ignorance will be a faded memory!

Ignorance is wisdom concealed

An illusion that forces the viewer to make it real

A corruption that alters appearance

Who said ignorance is bliss is a lover of ignorance

& What you love will love you in return

If you desire what is hidden from your eyes

It will manifest itself

What is revealed is a manifestation of someone else's creation/conception

Conception, birth and death is one big circle

Eventually all will return to its origin

If all that is revealed is a manifestation of someone else's conception

Then surely I am the manifestation of my creator's conception

Or am i an illusion appearing by a stroke of chance

How can I justify my existence?

If I cannot see my creator?

Surely it is because I exist in my creator's mind

And my creator exists in me

How else is it possible that I feel as I do?

How else is it that I love as I do?

How else is it that I feel pain, lust, and fear, joy, sorrow and peace?

How else is it that I feel hope, euphoria, shame, and victory, even life?

Where does an atom receive life?

Some say; its the invisible magnetic force binding its dense nucleus to the cloudy outer electrons

If I am alive, surely there is a reason for my existence

For what is an answer without a question?

And what use is a question without an answer?

We see the sun and say it serves a purpose

We see daylight and nighttime

And we concur that they serve a purpose

But we see ourselves and forget what purpose we serve

From whence has this ignorance manifested itself?

Why has my creator hidden itself from me?

Why has my creator left me to rely on the imaginations of another man?

Perhaps he desires to leave through me

To be recreated through me

Or perhaps he wishes to show me his everlasting love

To become my unconditional love

Love not based on the perceptions of my eyes but my heart

Spirit, Soul & Body

I have often pondered on the concept of spirit soul and body.

who is my spirit?

what is my soul?

and how does one sell his own soul?

i have beheld my body as one looking in a mirror

and often my mind has deceived me

often my mind has deceived itself

often my mind has conceived half baked truths

who is my mind and why does it speak so much

why does my spirit hide itself from me

where is my soul that i may redeem you with my love

All i see is my body

perhaps if i could see you too oh spirit & soul of mine

i would love you and feed you till you bloom and flourish

i heard a philosopher once say;

the brain is the throne of the spirit

the heart is the seat of the soul

and the mind is a mediator between the spirit soul and body

~ Selah

Finding the Almighty

In the Day of my reflection

my heart was heavily troubled

and i sought to behold the countenance of my God

To learn his true name and walk with him

I desired to be in his presence and sing love songs to him

for my heart craved after him

My spirit remembered the stories of old

how that Men walked with God

So i began to search for my God in the depths of an Extinct World

I heard the spirit of God whisper to me;

Search in the Words of the Resurrected One

still i took it upon myself that him i know,

but still i wish to know that which he raged against

that which he spoke of

that which he knew

as i searched and walked this path

'I stumbled upon the seeds planted by the enemy

and remembered the voice of my master saying

The kingdom of heaven is like unto a good man planting good seeds

and while he slept

the enemy planted tares'

as i began to examine these seeds,

Darkness and fear began to grow on me

Doubt consumed me,

and sickness consumed my flesh

I cried out,

MY lord my God why has thou forsaken me in the midst of a wicked generation

a generation where deception causes me to stumble

Then i heard the word of the Lord come to me saying

Wherefore has thou searched for thy God amongst a people

who rejected their God and brought upon themselves Judgement?

Behold Old things are passed and all things are become new

Know that ye are the Redeemed

Saved by grace

a SON OF GOD

and even in this day of judgement

the LORD your God speaks Loudly

therefore hold on to your confidence and do not waver

let the love in your Heart guide you

A letter to God

I have known you and loved you from my childhood

I have known you and loved non other but you

and even though a million times i have strayed

still i will seek your face night and day

i search for you because my heart longs for you

my soul aches for your presence

my spirit wants nothing else but to serve at your feet

but my heart is overthrown by sorrow

because though i know you, i cannot find all of you

the messages you sent me have been trampled on by selfish men with wicked hearts

the clues you left to lead me home have been inverted by a careless generation

my flesh has caused the words of your spirit to be muffled

and the enemy tests my faith in the truth

he makes me question and doubt the messages you have sent me

my vision is blurred

oh my love and master

where and how shall i find thee

i got your message about following the road called love

but the path is full of wicked men

how shall i walk this path without you by my side

Oh forgive me my Lord

I just remembered you are with me always'

and i need not look anywhere but believe

your spirit of truth bears witness with what is truth

Dear Dad

I wish i could see your face one more time

i wish i could tell you how my heart is breaking right now i wish i could hear your voice just for one more time

i wish you could hear me say; 'I'm sorry i wasn't there'

i'm sorry i didn't come to find you in time

i'm sorry is all i want to say

but all i have are wishes

i wish i could see your face one more time

just so i can tell you it ok

just so i can tell you; its gonna be ok

that your little girl made it

but all i can think of is: 'I'm Sorry'

I'm sorry i didn't say i love you

i'm sorry i wasn't there

i'm sorry i didn't make it to you in time

i'm sorry i don't know how to fill this gaping hole in my chest

i'm sorry i'm not sure how to carryon without you in the picture

i hope you found peace

i hope you found that beautiful place everyone talks about

i hope somehow wherever you are, you can see your baby girl did make it

that your baby girl is doing fine

i want to say goodbye

but i feel like i wasn't even given the chance to say hello but for now. I hope you Rest in Peace

BOOK 2

To Poetry With Love
By
Gloria Edokpa

It's been a While

It's been a while since I said I love you
It's been a while since I said I miss you
It's been a while since I heard your voice in the winds
It's been a while since I felt Goosebumps at the thought of you
It's been a while since my heart skipped a beat at the mention of your name
It's been a while since I got on my knees & sang love songs to you
It's been a while since I shed tears of love for you
It's been a while since I lifted these hands in awe of your beauty
Someone asked me today; do you know God?
And I replied; "I know GOD better than you do"
But then I realized
It's been a while since I felt you
It's been a while since I loved you dear LORD
It's been a while since I longed for you and I miss you my LORD

Lady of the Morning

Her beauty is more than I can bear
The lady in the morning
Venus is what they call her
Cos she twinkles in deep space
And her bright light is comparable to non-other

Isaiah called her the morning star
And spoke of her decent
Leaving many to ponder not just her identity
But the origin of her story

Grecia called her Aphrodite
Rome called her Venus
Goddess of love, beauty and sex
But I call her, 'lady of the morning'
For she's become a friend and a lover

I say good morning whenever I see her
I tell her my plans and wish her well for a beautiful day
I never cease to tell her how breathtakingly beautiful she is
and when the moon is present, I'll make a wish or two

I promised her a poem
To show her my love
And though she may not know
I'm blown away by her beauty

But just like many others
I fear she's enchanted my heart
Leaving me stuck in Lala land
Hoping I'll see her face again in the morning
Just so I can blow her a kiss and warm hello

Lady of the morning is what I call her
Because she's the most beautiful thing in the night sky

Scarlet Lover

Happy horrors in dreadful places,
Slow smiles and dark faces,
She hides hearts in deep bondage.
She's called the Scarlet lover.

A scarlet cord to bind the heartbreak
She stares in emptiness
And hopes for time travel
An awkward glance is strong enough to set things off
She's caught in a whirlwind of restless emotion
Nothing but intense passion is good enough

She dares not speak of her lust
How she longs for him like eve's forbidden fruit
She dares not think of those silent moans
That causes her floodgates to crumble
She dares not to remember him
For he's a careless lover
And enthusiasm was never his strength

Still, she bathes in mellow memories
Of a love she once forgot
But can't help but crave for more

They call her the scarlet lover
With a tattooed breast she suckles her lover
The queen of Sheba should be her name
Solomon's lover
A lover of wisdom and many mysteries
A deadly poison Suitable only for kings of the lost worlds

They call her the scarlet lover
Black is her color
And red is her obsession
Like fragile paintings her heart is her weakness
And mystery is her ecstasy

Come Hear Our Song

Beyond the dawn of glory
Enthralled in the Epiphany of hope
Lies our destiny surely
Once vivid now blurry
Once certain now bleak

We're the Children of a dead generation
The seeds of a forgotten tomorrow
And the Fruits of a forlorn aeon
Who will hear our story?

Our words are but faded fibers
Gone on the winds of wasted timelines
Lost with the hope of a dreary place
Once boisterous now solemn

We grasp and clutch to gilded fame
While holding on to weak strings of a broken song
But a tortured soul is all we've got to hold

Come hear us sing our song of hope
A Clarion call to those that see our obelisk glow
And when we've song the notes foretold
We'll see our lights burn through the night
And birth a new world of hope and faith

Lost

Funny faces in horrid chases
Like lowly hearts in holy places
We've lost our zeal for truthful stasis
Adorned with halos so tainted we crave humanity's crazes

We speak illusive truths and shroud subliminal messages in open spaces
Like forgotten lines of a terrible love song
Pelted on the faulty strings of an old and forlorn banjo
Our melody is that of pain and love in a web of twisted ashes
A heart so broken its pulse is made of fragile stitches.

What's mine is yours
And what's yours is mine
We trade lies like Iberian Vikings
Not knowing what truth's real face is

Our feeble minds, a canvass for the delusion that is society's paintbrush
Our blinded knowledge is ignorance personified in all its glory.
A steady flow of reality's blandness.
A wake up call would be but white noise.
A screeching sound from a frequency unknown.
Too sublime to be understood by all.

We've lost our touch with what's truly home.
Like the faded Hyde skin on a broken bass drum
Our song echoes on the waves of a deceptive mind bug
Clouding our sense of reality like the days of Nero and Caligula
We've built our home on the blood, tears and sweat of the weak ones
We've placed ourselves in exalted places and look to plunder foreign creases

I glare in disdain at your outspoken bigotry in the name of freedom
I stare in awe of you and your boundless ability to love in selfishness
Yet I mourn at your inability to comprehend the truth.
Selflessness, altruism, unconditional love, sacrifice, mercy, dedication, loyalty...
Words! Words I fear you may never understand
Words I know you will never comprehend

If I Could

If I could I would give you the world
But I can't so I'll give you my word
My heart and my love is all that I have
And today I'll lay it all at your feet
And hope this day you won't through it away
But even if you did I'll do it over and over again
For a moment to catch that glimpse of smile in your eyes
I'll love you always and forever
To the moon and back
To infinity and beyond
For eternity has not heard of our love
And history may never see this again

Find My Way Back

How do I start to find my way back home.
How do I start to hear you again amidst the noise & the chaos.
Where do i look to find my way back to you again.
Where do i look to find you again.
Where did i loose all of it.
How did I loose sight of you.
When did I get this lost!
Why cant I find my way back to you again!
Where do i find you again LORD.
How do I find you again LORD.
Help me find my way back home.
Help me find my way back to you.
For its in you I have a home!

Day Dreams

She stared into outer space
hoping to catch a glimpse of the gods she heard stories about as a child,
but all she saw were stars twinkling with so much beauty it was breathtaking.
She wondered if there was life out there.
If those who lived in those twinkling stars looked down every once in a while.
Her heart ached to live in faraway galaxies,
to be amongst the gods,
to explore the heavens,
to be one with the universe...
She wished to know the unknown,
to touch the stars.
To behold the beauty of the very essence of life.
If her heart could beat any faster, it would literally implode.
Suddenly she was startled by the loud horns of a passing train.
Suddenly, it was back to reality,
Back to the boring emptiness that is life on earth.
The pain of love
The aches of loneliness in a room full of people.
The bland taste of nothingness.

Same Evil, New Day

Today I sit and ponder.

Life seems to change

Yet everything remains the same

It's funny how time flies

and things appear to be different with every generation

But everything is the same

Just the same evil masked in a new costume.

All the people, all their thoughts

The Chaos, the Hatred

The greed, the love for life

The finger-pointing

The deception

The need to prove one's self right

It goes on and on

From generation to generation

Nothing really changes

Evil is reborn with a new name & a new face

They say there are no mistakes and we are our mistakes

and in every beginning there is an end

In unity there is chaos

Just as white light is made up of many colors

So humanity is made up of diverse people

If reality is a collection of varying Perceptions.

Why do we all collectively delude ourselves?

Pain

Pain in Passion

Passion in pain

I thought I loved

But then came the guilt

Stronger than the sharpest blade

Hurts more than a bleeding heart

I'm lost

Lost in you

My pain, my shame, my pleasure, my remorse

Once I loved

Now I hate

Love and hate

What's the difference

The pain I feel

is all I know

The remorse I bear

is all that's left

But then again

I'm not sure I would take it back

But I do hope

you feel my pain

For my love is you

And passion knows no bounds

Searching

I would die a thousand deaths

And Cross a million oceans

For the kisses of his lips

I would fight a dozen legions

Skip through 10,000 aeons

Take on all of Rameses' Army

Just to find my way back to him

But I'm lost

Lost in time and space

My heart searches for my love

To find him Is to find me

To find me is to find him

But where do I search

When life is a bottomless wormhole

He's my soul

He's my breath

He's that special moment I find bliss.

He's my life

He's my lover

He's my pain

My home

My heart

My helper

My bondsman

Then again, he's my illusion

And fiction never tasted better

A Perfect Dream

A perfect dream

He whispered with a kiss

The loving hunger

hidden with a smile

A warm embrace so kind

I swirl in heavenly emotions

Surrendering gently

To the throbbing pulse

Of a gentle, yet intense desire

Holding on to a dream once whispered

But slowly unfolding

Lovesick and high-strung

On a promise so fragile

Yet a certain hope

On the fingers of time soon to show

A quiet laughter

unveils a seductive smile

I'll gladly sing

Our uncharted song

With a tone so low

You'll barely know

A perfect dream

For you and I alone

Her Riddle

I searched high and low for her face

So familiar yet unknown

A dark show of dejavu

Once upon a dream

A lover's heart unfilled

A smokescreen to shade the pain

An illusive smile

Worn in hope for you

Slow to accept the truth

A fleeting thought of lust

Blossomed into love

A dreary twist in faith

Mine's not to hold

But to give and ask for none

To slightly anticipate her pain

Is to see into her being

The essence of her existence

So dark yet so beautiful

A hope for purple rain

A blue moon's destiny

Her face is a glimpse of hope

An unworthy blaze

Spun to hide the truth

Catching blue beats

On the pulse of a slow burning heart

Her love is mine to grasp

Her pain is mine to unfold

Her wisdom is mine to unveil

Like the riddles of a sphinx

The enigma of truth

The conundrum of a conscious heart

We Remember: A Poem Dedicated to the 9/11 Victims

On 9/11 we bore the pain

Caused by poisoned hearts and misguided minds

We faced the break and rise of a new form of hate

An emotion once unworthy of a second glance

Or a second of our precious time

But in an instant a vale was torn

Two worlds apart now consciously alert

The pain that's left is more than we can bear

It's left our lips quivering and quaking

Like queasy guts on a homeless nymph

Lost and threatened on a frosty cold island by a chimerical beast

The gash that's left is a hole that can't be filled

But we love despite the emptiness and pain

A meaningless hope lingers at the aftermath and years after

Like red rain descending on the Egyptian Nile

In an age that is as clueless as a blank canvass

We remember you today while fighting our tears and fears

Knowing not whence comes our strength and determination

We remember you this day with hope and unflinching fervor

With optimism for a better tomorrow

We remember

Cos you are the essence of our hope

A world were love reigns supreme

Dear October

Dear October

September's gone and she was mighty kind to me.

She left me with a few loose change and a warm heart full of hope and anticipation.

She wasn't always kind but she's the first of the ember months so what can i say?

I love to see her every now and again, but it's you i love even more.

November's ok and December's even better

but i love you the more for leading me on my autumn lover.

If i sing you a song, would you love me any better than September?

Because i did write you a love letter but it's hidden in my heart.

Besides, the full moon's here, so what could be better?

I hold you in my heart not knowing what you'll become.

But i do hope you'll treat me well my autumn lover

For my heart is broken at the thought of your many lovers

But who am I to love the second of an ember

If you will be my libra, let me be your Scorpio

For days, months and years are nothing but our own creation

Yet I love you October and I know not why

Then again maybe not

Hi October

Did you miss me?

Emotional Abuse

Emotional Abuse

It goes on and on

The abuse

The accusations

His need to make her see her faults

His need to make her feel less than adequate

The constant snooping through her things

The constant fighting

Where does it end

How far is too far

A selfish love

With no room to break free

She says; 'let me go'

But He changes for a little while

Soon enough, it's back to square one

The mood swings

Angry mornings

Unemotional evenings

A lonely lovers pain is her solace

Having none to talk to

Having none to understand

Having none to share with

Yet he asks her; why do you hide?

What is hidden?

What's the point?

They go on and on

Cleaving to the path of a broken road

2 strangers clinging on to fragile strings

Not knowing how to let go

Who's wrong?

Who's right?

Or does it even matter?

Does love run empty?

What happens to empty hearts?

And untrusting lovers?

Where do the loveless ones end up?

His abuse is her emotion

Her emotion is his burden

Her heart has become homeless

And Emptiness is her hope

Two lovers gone astray

With no hope of return

But broken threads

And forlorn bonds

I see you

We are all alike

All of us together

The greed

The hunger

We crave the bad

Yet act the good

I hear her voice

The old lady

Who whimpers

And wonders when it all ends

Her eyes are set on other worlds

Not visible to the young ones

She looks on with anticipation

Thinking any moment now

The aches and pain

Hopefully will cease

The loneliness

Hopefully would be gone

She closes her eyes

And makes a wish upon death

I hear her screams

The little child

Whose mother is nowhere to be found

And the monster above her

Is devoid of a conscience

A demon in daylight

An animal with opportunity

Opportunity to prey

Slowly her screams become whimpers

The pain slowly tears through her innocent nerves

Sucking the little life out her

I hear her gasp for her last breath

Her tiny heart stops

I hear his cries for help

The young man

Beaten to a pulp

His face, bloody and broken

His flesh, slowly burning

He's burnt to death

For reasons he knows not why

The pain is numbing

Soon it's over

And all he remembers is

"Where is my helper?

My faith is lost"

I feel his aching heart

The old man

Whose lover is no more

He longs to be with her

The loneliness is heart wrenching

There's no one to take away the pain

No one to call home

Her absence hurts more than a million knives

I hear her

The woman whose lost her child

Her pain is more than she can bear

Her heart bleeds blue

None can comfort her

I see you

I see your pain

It's my burden

I see you

I see your inability to be perceptive

I see you've gone cold

I see your heart's rid itself of passion

I see you and I wonder why

This is my burden

This is my curse

This is my pain

Hope in a hopeless age

Love in a loveless aeon

Passion in a brutal world

Chaos is my solace

My heart still wanders

Still! Who can lift a wanderer's curse?

Number 3

The law of dualism

Good vs evil

Right vs wrong

They say it's either this or that

The dualist mentality

Did it all begin with Descartes' theory of Dualism

Or did Descartes simply deduce the theory of dualism from human observation?

Welcome to trialism I here

It's white, black & grey areas

The Trinity

The Triad

Did it begin with ancient Sumeria through Egypt then Greece

Or was it a deduction from the metaphysical?

Trialism I hear

Trialism I see

Say hello to #3

For 2 is no more & 3 is 1

The 3rd person

Unseen but most dominant.

White and black are puppets

But Grey is your puppet

& your puppeteer

Number 3 is his name

But he's really the only one

And while everyone looks to # 1 & #2

#3 leaves them confused

Because he was never in the original picture to begin with

He only shows up in subliminal messages

Too subtle for the feeble ones to perceive

Too confusing for most

What's worse is, he's both 1 & 2

But neither #1 or #2 are #3

3 kinds of hunger

3 kinds of people

3 questions

2 choices

1 answer

#3 is your answer

But be careful for it's not the #3 that is seen

Shrouded in the invisibility cloak that is 'the Other' aka 'everyone else'

#3 is hidden in the 12th house

But #12 gave #3 to #6

And #6 is not who you think he is

#3 is your answer

And Eventually only # 3 defines eternity

But to discover #3 is both damnation & redemption

Because 3 was built to be your illusion and your reality

That your judgement may be justified by you alone!

And your punishment wroth on you by your own hands!

Yes #3 is your answer

But it is not the #3 you know

Neither is it the #3 you think

We haven't always remembered

Blurred wishes gliding on the ascent of pivotal moments

Rousing the perfect fires in our deepest emotions

hearts pounding like gentle lovers wrapped in passion

our voices echo loudly in medleys of unsung heroes

knowing this enigma is nothing but faded glories

and subprime loans in the hands of Predatory lenders

we haven't always remembered

yet we haven't always had amnesia

between love and lust, our spirits wade through the halls of shallow valleys

knowing not whence comes our beat

or our queue for spiritual wakening

we thread lightly on magic carpets

and hope on dying stars for solemn moments

We weren't always this lost

yet we haven't always found our way through time

Our hope's on imaginary beings

longing for lullabies and empty promises

like prometheus our creativity is treachery

and social delusion has left us with perfidy

Mind control like traders and derivatives

we've lost a hold on these our liberties

freedom of speech freedom of thought

but freedom's never come cheap

and what's my freedom is your captivity

but never again we hope

never again will we be led astray

and when it's all said and done

and all's done that's been said

and history repeats itself

because we've failed once again to remember

even then and above all else

will my love for you prevail

Six and Six-Smiths

Eternal recurrence

I have been here before

Once upon a dejavu

As a six-smith

Bound to the sixth house

In Middle summers

When date fruits bloom

I heard her say;

"Our lives are not our own

We are bound to others

Past, present and future

And by every crime or act of kindness

We birth our future"

And i understood her.

Her voice so clear and familiar

It was a clarion call for one

Like a perfect symphony sextet

Her face is June in Gemini

And she should be the third

But the Romans turned back time

And made her 6

But Judah keeps her still in her proper place

Lowly and twisted

Intense and extreme

A twin with herself

Naphtali should be her name

But that was a long time ago

Before a million kings plundered her home

And evil men sort her thrown

Her words are alive

Wisdom is in her courts

And knowledge abides in her bosom

So I listen closely

As she whispers;

"Knowledge is a mirror

To see who we were

And who we might become"

That we may no longer

Ask the 'what' but the 'why'

Like; Why do we keep making the same mistakes over and over again?

Why does unanimity seem impossible?

And why can't I just love you forever

Her message is nirvana

But she must save her own

For her SOS is only as strong as the weak ones

And her hope is not for this day

Still she will call

And when she does

Be able to hear

And be able to understand

It's Not You

I look into your eyes and realize

My love for you is but a fairy tale

For the one I love is non existent

And the person I want to love

isn't you

I cling to hopeless memories

Wondering if you love me too

But nothing ever gets answered whilst being wondered

It all started with a smile

A gentle kiss and a warm embrace

Then it was you

You became my smile

My escape

My safe place

To dream

To smile

To love like crazy once again

But then I realized

It wasn't you

For the one I love is non existent

And the one I want to love

Isn't you

It was once upon a mistake

It started with a bold question

A truth or dare

A questionable passion

To have and to hold

What wasn't ours

We dared and we lied

But then I realized

It wasn't you

For the one I love is non existent

& The one I want to love

Isn't you

You are my inspiration and my passion

You will always be my smile

My love

My safe place

My beautiful illusion

And the one I'll love deeply

But I realize

It wasn't you

For you haven't loved me too

And I haven't been a fair lover

Yet this mythical love affair

Was the best in neverland

My Forbidden Fruit

His eyes are the perfect river

A blinding ray of exquisite sun down

Firm yet soft as moonlight at dusk

His lips were made to be craved

The pinnings of a hopeless heart

My sub-conscious hope for a perfect lover

An imperfectly perfect ecstasy

To want him is to long for pain

To have him is nothing but euphoria

A blissful moment in heaven

A lovers dreamland

Like Oliver, I'm left begging for more

For an exhilarating moment in eternity

One more moment only doomed for heart ache

One second to utopia

I wish only if he were mine

Mine to have, to keep and to hold

Not just for a moment in time

But for never ending

Like cinderella's Prince Charming

But then again, if he was mine to keep

He wouldn't be my forbidden fruit

And we don't really know what happened to Prince Charming now, do we?

November

Snowflakes and cold winds

In comfy cottages

North of the western kingdoms

My November is home again

And though you might soon go away

My heart is warm for now till then

Bring me teacups and biscuits

For my love has fully blossomed

To find warmth within the walls of your heart

Is all I ask of thee oh November

For the high seasons and thankful moments

Are all but yours to bring

Bring me turkey bring me roast

For thanksgiving is here again

And when we say our prayers together again

I'll be sure to say thanks for you

Hold me close and bring on December

But be sure to let January know

For scorpio's wrath is a little too scary to bare

And Sagittarius knows to aim for my heart

But oh November my November

Do treat me well

For I'm a lover not a fighter

And my love runs deeper than the Euphrates rivers

My Scorpio Clan

Hidden faraway

In middle-eastern stars

Beneath mystery & intoxicating passion

do my scorpions stand steady and supreme

to teach you humility

The will to fight

And The choice to believe

Like the clear sounds of a Beacon call

The cries of victory

The beginning of change

Like Columbus and the Indians

Like Water displacement & Tsunami buoys

My scorpions do go forth to conquer

Riddled with power

Astute, highly intelligent & determined

The scorpions stay fixed as leaders in the eight house

Reserved, loyal, firm & somewhat proud

It is said; The wisdom of the serpent lies concealed in scorpius

With a destiny only for greatness

Let her rule these lands

For though her passion be stronger than wine

And her wrath be fiercer than the snakes venom

she was truly born to lead

And if I find her love addictive

Then leave me be

For this drunken man has found his solace

A million stings for his kisses

Let him rule my heart

For my scorpion king knows me too well

And though I may be drunk off his venom

Let me stay drunk with his love

For passion was made to be this way

Then again, if I wake up broken hearted

Leave me be

Cos I'll gladly take one more sip from his fountain

My Obsession

My addiction

My obsession

Would you love me like I wanted to be loved

Would you be my obsession

& let me be your addiction

Let our love be the drug that gods crave

Let my heart be the treasure that you pillage

Like a barbarian warlock

Could you love me with aggression

Or like a Greco-roman soldier

Would you plunder my nether regions?

Better yet, Like Romeo and Juliet

Would you make passionate love to me

Like our last breath depended on it?

Make me beg and mourn for you

Like a lost junkie high on love

For I am an obsessive lover

Sex is my drug and love is my addiction

Goodbye December

Goodbye my dear December

Last of the embers and my favorite member

Your yuletide I'll be sure to remember

When autumn comes around with a bender

Say hi to November

October and September

Lost love and memories misremembered

From calendars ditched in attics and dustpans

Remember my December

That Santa makes you special

And good kids look to your return like Eastenders and Air Benders

But oh December my December

When you return next calendar

I'll be here singing love songs

And mending hearts pumped with endorphins

So be sure to bring me more glad tidings

To make my heart merrier than bartenders with lavenders and high spenders

Goodbye December

Goodbye 2012

Thank you for all the many blessings

A Birthday Poem for my Friend Star

Memories scream somehow through you Beautiful Star

Sharing surprises and prospects with every warm smile

Every gentle word and every story untold

Let's hide together on silent nights

Underneath pitch black blue skies

And a million twinkling stars

We'll call on the gods to come hear our stories

And carry the songs of our hearts through the milky-way

A simple song for a Star

A million wishes upon you

My beautiful Scorpio

Tis your birthday

So let us be merry

For the angels know this day

And the heavens know your name all too well

Forceful and determined

Emotional and intuitive

Powerful and passionate

Exciting and magnetic

A beautiful Star born to soar

Just like Kelly says

I believe you can fly

Happy Birthday Star!!!